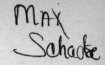

THIS BOOK HAS
SOMETHING SPECIAL TO SAY TO
EACH PERSON WHO READS IT.

The Lazy Man's Guide to Enlightenment is unique
because it allows each person to find his or her own
way. There are no strict rules. No daily regimen.
Just a handful of simple reminders. It is most defi-
nitely a book for everyone.

The Lazy Man's Guide to Enlightenment was originally
printed and published by the author himself. The
first printing was sold out in two months. The own-
ers of a small bookstore in California liked the book
so much that they started their own publishing com-
pany to handle the thousands of requests for the
Guide—often from original buyers who had given
their copies away as gifts. Now, with the Bantam
edition, everyone can experience the phenomenon
that has already brightened nearly a quarter of a
million lives.

ABOUT THE AUTHOR

THADDEUS GOLAS came upon the idea for *The Lazy Man's Guide to Enlightenment* back in 1952, when he decided to try to listen to God instead of praying to him. As a boy, he worked as a printer's apprentice, later graduated from Columbia University and held various jobs in publishing. *The Guide* was actually written after the author "plunged into psychedelic chaos in San Francisco for several years." While he has received numerous letters from fans of his book, Mr. Golas has never lectured or held classes on it. Mr. Golas is presently living in Humboldt County, California.

The Lazy Man's
Guide to
Enlightenment

by Thaddeus Golas

BANTAM BOOKS

TORONTO · NEW YORK · LONDON · SYDNEY · AUCKLAND

THE LAZY MAN'S GUIDE TO ENLIGHTENMENT
*A Bantam Book / published by arrangement with
Seed Center*

PRINTING HISTORY
*Originally published by the author in 1972
Seed Center edition published November 1972
7 printings through 1979
Bantam edition / June 1980
2nd printing . . . July 1981*

ISBN   0-553-20440-8

Published simultaneously in the United States and Canada

---

*Bantam Books are published by Bantam Books, Inc. Its trademark, consisting
of the words "Bantam Books" and the portrayal of a bantam, is Registered
in U.S. Patent and Trademark Office and in other countries. Marca Registrada.
Bantam Books, Inc., 666 Fifth Avenue, New York, New York 10103.*

PRINTED IN THE UNITED STATES OF AMERICA

11   10   9   8   7   6   5

Contents

Foreword   9

Who are we?   13

Look, Ma, I'm Enlightened   22

How to feel good   30

Lifesavers   35

How we got here   39

Self-improvement   46

Time and vibrations   53

Going through changes   58

What is real?   65

How you get there   72

A Fable   78

Even Lazier   79

Foreword

I am a lazy man. Laziness keeps me from believing that enlightenment demands effort, discipline, strict diet, non-smoking, and other evidences of virtue. That's about the worst heresy I could propose, but I have to be honest before I can be reverent. I am doing the work of writing this book to save myself the trouble of talking about it.

There is an odd chance that this is what someone needs to read in order to feel better about himself. If you are a kind person and want to know what to expect when enlightenment strikes and why it comes to you, with or without psychedelic help, this is for you.

These are the rules of the game as I see them. I realize that many of us are opening up very fast these days, and one of the most common delusions we face is the belief that our sense of revelation is unique. The feeling of knowing the truth is not enough. My intention is not to pretend final truth, but to suggest certain simple attitudes that will work for anybody and stay with you in the most extreme freak-out or space-out, even when your mind is completely blown. These attitudes are so simple that I'm surrounding them with a picture of the universe to show why they work even when you don't believe they will.

The universe is so vast and complex that if we needed books like this to become enlightened, we'd never make it. But on the other hand the universe is so simple in design that there's no reason for anyone to be puzzled or unhappy. It's easy to control your existence, no matter how complicated it looks. I've abandoned the idea of writing this a number of times, on the ground that people didn't know it because they didn't want to. But in the end there is no more reason for not writing it than there is for writing it.

I am writing what I will want to read someday when I am stuck in a weird place. Several times on bummers I've thought: What could I say to someone in this state of mind that would mean anything? That's the kind of testing this information has had. There isn't a line in this book that is there just because it sounds beautiful. The information is practical and reliable. It has taken me and others safely through some extreme states of mind, and can be reduced to a few phrases that are simple enough to recall in any crisis.

The first chapter begins with a briefly stated idea about how the universe is made, and the rest of the book discusses our lives from that viewpoint. It is a far-reaching idea, extending into every field of knowledge, and since it took me many years to get it straight, I cannot expect that anyone else should casually accept it. All I can do is ask that you play the idea game, see where it leads, and check it out against what you know. What has to be true for the universe to look to us as it does? Is there a credible bridge between matter and spirit? Like many people, I wrestled with such concerns for years, and this book contains some of the conclusions. Perhaps these conclusions will be meaningful to you only if you follow your own process of checking and proving. If so, the first chapter contains all you will need to keep you busy for a long time. On the other hand, if all you want is a handy trip guide, you'll find that, too.

I'm really not expecting anyone to take these sentences and expand them again into a feeling of realization. But if one of you whom I never hear about gets a little higher and happier, then I would write all this again a thousand times over. I hope you find the vibrations pleasant.

CHAPTER ONE
Who are we?

We are equal beings and the universe is our relations with each other. The universe is made of one kind of entity: each one is alive, each determines the course of his own existence.

That is really all you need to know to understand this book or write your own. Everything I say has its roots in that first paragraph, and it is possible to resolve any question by going back to it and thinking it through for yourself.

The universe is made of one kind of whatever-it-is, which cannot be defined. For our purpose, it isn't necessary to try to define it. All we need to do is assume that there is only *one kind* of whatever-it-is, and see if it leads to a reasonable explanation for the world as we know it.

The basic function of each being is expanding and contracting. Expanded beings are permeative; contracted beings are dense and impermeative. Therefore each of us, alone or in combination, may appear as space, energy, or mass, depending on the ratio of expansion to contraction chosen, and what kind of vibrations each of us expresses by alternating expansion and contraction. Each being controls his own vibrations.

A completely expanded being is space. Since expansion is permeative, we can be in the "same space" with one or more other expanded beings. In fact, it is possible for all the entities in the universe to be one space.

We experience expansion as awareness, comprehension, understanding, or whatever we wish to call it. When we are completely expanded, we have a feeling of total awareness, of being one with all life. At that level we have no resistance to any vibrations or interactions of other beings. It is timeless bliss, with unlimited choice of consciousness, perception, and feeling.

Space is a level of experience that any of us can reach, but it is difficult to talk about on our present plane precisely because it is unlimited. It is that which chooses limits and makes definitions. We might say: all experiences are available to the One Mind, and the One Mind is all of us or any of us at the highest level of expansion. Or we might theorize: God could not create anything more limited than Himself that would persist, but if He duplicates Himself, He can enjoy a persistent universe. Each entity, therefore, is a duplicate of God, "made in His image."

It doesn't matter what words we use: we exist and the universe exists, and it is possible to test this expansion-contraction idea within the limited scope of what is real to us as human beings, especially in atomic and sub-atomic studies.

When a being is totally contracted, he is a mass particle, completely imploded. To the degree that he is contracted, a being is unable to be in the same space with others, so contraction is felt as fear, pain, unconsciousness, ignorance, hatred, evil, and a whole host of strange feelings. At an extreme he has the feeling of being completely insane, of resisting everyone and everything, of being unable to choose the content of his consciousness. Of course, these are just the feelings appropriate to mass vibration levels, and he can get out of them at any time by expanding, by letting go of all resistance to what he thinks, sees, or feels.

When a being is alternating expansion and contraction, he is energy. My guess is that at the middle point, fifty percent expansion and fifty percent contraction, a being would be logical, non-subjective, egoless, and predictable. This may be the "zero" which is one side of energy equations in physics, as well as the "ego-death" we go through in expanding to higher levels of awareness.

It is important to note that energy is not a quantity of anything "objective." Energy, like space and matter, is what a lot of live beings are doing. Energy beings usually react to their neighbors in a way that is often predictable and apparently automatic, like falling dominoes. While relating to space beings, energy beings will appear to be high, vibrating rapidly, with a sense of increasing subjective freedom. Oriented to mass beings, they will be low energy, vibrating more slowly with a growing feeling of subjective compulsion and disorder.

The universe is an infinite harmony of vibrating beings in an elaborate range of expansion-contraction ratios, frequency modulations, and so forth.

There is a particular set of feelings and ideas that goes with every variation, every combination, every vibration level. There is also a different perception of how other beings are relating from every different viewpoint. The thought of these possibilities is so staggering, trying to contain them in writing is so ridiculous, that it is hard for me to move my pen any further. However, what we are after is to isolate some basic attitudes that will recover awareness of our freedom to move around in this maze—or go straight to the top.

What we need to remember is that there is nobody here but us chickens. The entire universe is made of beings just like ourselves. Every particle in every atom is a live being. Every molecule or cell is a tribe of beings. Energy is a large number of us vibrating together. Space is an infinite number of our brothers and sisters in perfect bliss.

There is no important difference between live and dead matter, since both are made up of live entities. Not only is mass convertible into energy, but energy is convertible into space, and vice versa. It is our own withdrawal from awareness, our own mass condition, that makes us see our brothers and sisters as objective matter, energy, and space. We always have the experiences and perceptions appropriate to our vibration level.

The same rules apply to all of us. The rules do not come from anywhere outside ourselves. They come from the truth that we are all equal, we all have the same range of possible behavior and experience. We are free to do anything we want to do, within the necessary laws of our relations as equal beings. And love must be the first law. Love is the *action* of being in the same space with other beings, which means that love is real, as real as we are. Love is not a limited idea, it is something we do, ultimately with our whole selves.

Perhaps many of us do not like it where we are in the universe now, but we can all be certain that we got where we are by our own decisions to expand in love or withdraw from it.

The kind of brain and body you have, the family and society, the time in history you were born into, all these and more were determined by you yourself, by your degree of expansion, by your willingness to love. No one did anything to you. No one forced you. There is absolute justice in the experience that each of us is having every second of the day. In one sense we can all relax, because nothing is secret, nothing is lost, nothing is forgotten, no one is abandoned.

Each of us is the same kind of being, capable of outflowing attention and awareness, or withdrawing it. And that is all we need to do: Give full, permissive, loving attention to absolutely anything that we see in our minds, in our bodies, in our environment, in other people.

Expansion in love is an action that is available to every being in the universe all the time. A willing awareness will take us to heaven, a loving attitude will make us free. Nothing else controls our fate. Good or bad behavior is secondary. Whatever you are doing, love yourself for doing it. Whatever you are thinking, love yourself for thinking it. Love is the only dimension that needs to be changed. If you are not sure how it feels to be loving, love yourself for not being sure of how it feels. There is nothing on earth more important than the love which conscious beings feel towards each other, whether or not it is ever expressed.

There is no point in worry or wonder about worse or better spiritual conditions, although that game is available. You will not be able to rise above your present vibration level to stay until you love the way you are now.

No matter what your spiritual condition is, no matter where you find yourself in the universe, your choice is always the same: to expand your awareness or contract it. And you have to start where you are. There is nothing wrong with being where you are—it's one of the infinite experiences available to us. What you are, I can be. What I am, you can be.

Whatever we have done in withdrawing from full consciousness of the One Mind, we are doing now. Whatever we are doing will always be within us to do, even when we are not doing it, and therefore is not to be resisted, but transcended. These are reminders I frequently use: *"That's always within me." "This, too, can be known with a fully expanded awareness."*

We can trust the flow of the universe. If these rules of love are true, then they are effective whether we agree with them or not, whether we are conscious of them or not, whether or not we use words to talk about them. The reality of love is something you do for yourself, with or without words, and judge the results from your own experiences. All information like this exists in space all the time, and doesn't need books for its reality. It's always within you.

It follows that I am not writing this book out of any sense of objection to what anyone believes now. Beyond all reason is the mystery of love: you know we are all equal, no one in truth needs any help from anyone else, no one needs to be told anything or given anything—and then you do the most compassionate act anyway, do the best for your brothers and sisters that you have in you. I'm relaying what was given to me when I felt I needed it: if I felt that way, maybe someone else does, too. This is a letter to my brothers and sisters, a love note to try to show how, when we thought love wasn't working, it was working perfectly.

It's an interesting mental exercise to turn the whole game upside down: the problem is not how to free yourself from the mass level, how to get enlightened. The real question is: If you are a completely free and self-determined being, how did you lock yourself into a body to play games on the material plane? How did you get yourself and others to agree to this game? How did you get it to be compulsive?

Several times when I've spaced out, I flashed: Well, if it's that easy to get out, I might as well go back and play the game. Maybe that's the ultimate temptation. And maybe no one really wants to know how easy it is, nobody wants to upset the game. We may all be playing let's pretend, hide-and-seek.

Physical reality is one of the biggest horror movies of all, and you know how we love horror movies. If the universe as we see it from our vibration level is illusory, only partially true, then that's all the more reason for enjoying it and loving it, instead of getting freaked by it.

Everything that happens on earth can be experienced on any of thousands of different vibration levels, from the most euphoric to the gloomiest. We are entirely free to emphasize any level we wish. We need change nothing but our own attention and love, our own expansion and love.

Since the universe is nothing but live beings, each controlling his own level and his own relationships, there is absolutely nothing in the universe that needs to be corrected in any way. We don't have to do anything about it, whatever it is. There is consciousness everywhere in the universe, and we can trust all beings to handle their own decisions. No matter how it looks to us, love never loses control: the laws of our relations are as honest and exact as the laws of physics.

I can't say I know at this moment what all these laws are. But on some level everybody knows that we are all getting exactly what we deserve.

The harmony is infinite and one and divine. Where do you figure you fit into it? Don't be too hard on yourself. A little bit of love goes a long way.

CHAPTER TWO

Look, Ma, I'm Enlightened

What do you do to become enlightened? What
are the signs that you are succeeding? How
does your life change as you become more
enlightened?

*There is nothing you need to do first in
order to be enlightened.*

All potential experiences are within you
already. You can open up to them at any
time, faster than instantaneously, just by
being there.

But there's no hurry. Total expansion is
always there, beyond time, within and around
you. You need only open your awareness at
the pace you find safe and comfortable. If
LSD is too fast, go slower. This is home. We
all belong in the universe.

Nothing gets in our way, but most of us
are likely to open up in stages, gradually. We
tend to go up in cycles of emotion: after
each burst of euphoric realization, we may hit
a new and different kind of negativity, the
next thing we need to learn to love. But the
higher you go, the easier it gets.

The experience of complete awareness,
being space, does not mean being presently

conscious of every detail in the universe, every possible relationship between limited, withdrawn entities. Being space is a *readiness* to be aware fully of anything conceivable. It means we have no resistance, no denial of any concept or relationship. Therefore, to achieve enlightenment, we are not required to gather any particular set of ideas or experiences, virtues or sufferings. Anything that exists can be experienced with a completely expanded awareness.

Regardless of how you have limited your awareness, you are a free and self-determined being. No other live being, nor any group of beings, can control your vibration level. So there is nothing in the universe, especially the physical part of it, that can counter your free will.

That means that the physical world has no power over you whatsoever: it doesn't tempt you, it doesn't corrupt you, it doesn't get in the way of enlightenment, "it" doesn't do anything to you.

You are the sole cause of your level of existence. Your internal condition is never programmed. The experience of being forced or controlled against your will can occur only when you make yourself dense, when you contract your awareness.

Our reality at any level consists of whatever unique conscious beings we perceive as alive, and the process of enlightenment is expanding our comprehension of other beings, until we experience everything as a live inter-action.

The more we withdraw from loving other beings, the more of a "physical" world we will contend with, the more mass-obsessed we become. On the other hand, the more we open up to our brothers and sisters, the less solid the world becomes.

Enlightenment is any experience of expanding our consciousness beyond its present limits. We could also say that perfect enlightenment is realizing that we have no limits at all, and that the entire universe is alive.

The difficulty in writing about it, and in all efforts to tell how to achieve it, comes of trying to use limited terms to talk about going beyond limits. To be enlightened is to be in a state of flexible awareness, an open mind. Enlightenment is the very process of expand-ing, not of arriving at a different set of limits.

There is no one correct way of looking at life "after" enlightenment. We are not obliged to be or not be anything, as long as in our hearts and minds we are whole.

What does it mean, to be whole? It means that we must be willing to conceive of, to contain within ourselves, whatever is "other than" any limited idea. It means knowing that when we emphasize a positive, we are at the same time creating a negative. When we choose an ideal of knowledge, then we must deal with the ignorance that is *other than* the knowledge. When we emphasize an ideal of holiness, then we must live with the sin that is its companion, and accept our responsibility for having created it.

If we deny doing so, that is a contraction of awareness; we become dense, we become mass-level entities, we are incarnated in physical bodies. And we cannot control what we have denied creating, it is forced into our attention whether we like it or not, and so we live in a world of sin and ignorance.

However, if we remain constantly open and unresisting to such negatives, we are not compelled to dwell on them: If we allow that ugliness is always within us, then we are free to create beauty. If we know that stupidity is always within us, then we are free to emphasize this intelligence.

Love is the highest and holiest action because it always contains that which is not love within itself, it always and ever moves to include the unloving.

How often we try to figure out a cause-and-effect sequence in our experiences, when what is happening is merely a swing of alternating conditions. We may choose a negative task, like monastic discipline, and then feel rewarded. Or conversely, we may pursue a seductive pleasure, and then feel cheated. We never stand back to see that we are just swinging like pendulums.

And many of us insist on thinking of ourselves as only kind, good, and wise: we try to be pendulums that swing only to one side.

The remedy for this confusion is to be loving, to experience life without mental resistance, until we rise above mass and energy to the space level. On that level, where love is constant and our awareness is open, we will more easily comprehend the miracle of containing contradictions, opposites, and paradoxes. We will be free to experience what we choose, because we will not deny that we always contain everything *other than* our choice. Karma is not "paying for" exactly what you did in the past. It's just that, as you raise your vibration level, you may encounter the *kind* of experiences you withdrew from in the past, or you may run into anything *other than* what you are insisting on now. If you try to close your mind, you will drop back to a lower vibration. But if you look calmly at undesired events, absorb them mentally, and *love yourself for disliking them*, you will keep going higher. You might say that for a while you must take your bum trip with your high.

As you deal with and love each new disturbing phenomenon, you will begin to realize that none of the threatening evil that bothered you has disappeared from the world. But your compulsive feelings of dismay and helplessness will be gone, you will learn how to steer your way around or through turbulent vibrations, and in time they won't happen to you any more. You will see how you can change your emotions and experiences by understanding their relation to your awareness level.

For instance, if your feelings fade after a deeply loving experience with someone (which is especially likely if you were high on marijuana or LSD at the time), you can understand it as a fading out of being in the same space now that you are both vibrating on a lower level again. When you know that, and know that the low mood can pass just as easily as it came on, then you are less likely to make big decisions and get into arguments because of it. You just relax your mind and watch it go by.

Currently many of us are experiencing temporary highs and flashes of illumination, especially with psychedelics available. If things get weird in new ways after such euphoric times, you need not be disturbed. It may be a sign you're going higher still.

Meanwhile we should realize that we tend to return to the vibration level where we feel stable, something we can "live with." It's the level of stability, the level where we feel ourselves to be comfortably on the same vibration with others, that needs to be changed. And that can be done only through an unresisting state of mind, a constantly expanding love.

It is quite natural, in pursuing enlightenment or just in trying to be happier, to look to your everyday experiences for signs of results. Indeed, your daily life is nothing else but an expression of your spiritual condition. Your life will change as you become more loving, but not in ways that you can exactly predict. What happens is not as important as how you react to what happens.

There is a good attitude to take towards any goal: It's nice if it happens, nice if it doesn't. Long before you get to where you can confidently make choices for the future, you may find that you are no longer interested in predicting much. You won't mind letting go of one beautiful experience because love will make the next one just as rewarding.

Similarly there isn't much specific advice to be given about what enlightened existence should be on Earth, and I am reluctant to make glowing predictions about what is possible. As we have seen, as soon as we are completely willing to create a condition, it changes into something else if our minds are blocked to alternatives. On our mass level, that "something else" is often likely to be unpleasant, and as soon as we try to withdraw from our feelings about it, we are stuck with it. That's one way to explain why ideal and beautiful events vanish from our lives, and bad and dull ones last, and the same applies in predicting a rosy future.

But no matter how vague and unwieldy that process seems, love will overcome it. It can be safely predicted that, as you grow more loving of yourself and others, you will in this lifetime begin seeing every person and object as a perfect form, just the way they are now. You will feel a rich pleasure in every moment. And since beauty really is in the eye of the beholder, your vibrations will be beautiful, too.

CHAPTER THREE

How to feel good

It's all right to have a good time. That's one of the most important messages of enlightenment.

We should try to comprehend the highest pleasure level, the pleasure of God, so to speak, in all that we perceive. No one in higher consciousness wants any of us to have a miserable time on earth.

There is a paradise in and around you right now, and to be there you don't even have to make a move, not even lifting your eyes from this page. You can open yourself to the diamondlike perfection of everything you see and feel. If you don't think it can happen that easily, just be loving, moment by moment, and trust that it will come to you.

No one on the space level ever puts barriers or tests in the way of someone who is trying to raise his spiritual level. Hindsight may make it look as though you were being tested, but in truth you are always being allowed to decide for yourself, to define the universe that is real to you.

Higher beings are only too happy when you show yourself loving enough to rise. You will be given every help and chance when you ask for it, whether you ask by taking LSD or any other way, be it simple prayer or writing a letter to Santa Claus. You are never asked to torment or frustrate yourself. You don't have to prove anything. You *can't* prove anything: your vibrations always speak true, you can't lie about them.

And it is easy to rise on the wings of love. No matter how convincing any perception of any level of reality, no matter how overwhelming, intricate and complex, you are still seeing only a fragment within our true reality: being just us, unresisting, unattached, loving all.

It is also all right to have a good time in sexual relations. In truth, a satisfying orgasm is a spiritual realization more than a technical accomplishment. The flesh is not apart from the spirit. The body is an ecstatic creation of many beings vibrating on other levels of consciousness. A deep orgasm is a realization of love on many levels, including those which many of us now think of as "animal." Love, getting into the same space or on the same vibration with others, is the ground of our being, and takes an infinity of forms. As in all other experiences, we always have the sexual experiences we deserve, depending on our loving kindness towards ourselves and others.

The ecstasy of sex can be considered a mirror to our psychic dissolution in the space of our divine brothers and sisters in the higher levels of expansion. Making love is one demonstration of how space relations ask us to surrender in love, and absorb the differences and imperfections and beauties of other beings.

If this is so, why is asceticism so often recommended as a spiritual path, and why does it sometimes appear to work? As we saw in the preceding chapter, when you push hard in one direction, you are likely to be swung into a state other than what you intend. When you insist on having only sensual pleasure, you will, unless your mind is open, be thrown into a state where asceticism seems like the right course. And when you go far enough in asceticism, you may be thrown into bliss and ecstasy, as many saints have told us.

Also, if you complain loud enough, you will be given a flash of insight into higher consciousness. If you deny yourself food, sex, communication, or sleep, you are in a way reporting to headquarters that your life form isn't working, and you may be allowed a brief return to space to check it out. But such flashes, though they presently make up most of what humanity knows of space, are not the entire light, no matter how convincing they feel. And these flashes are unstable, they are not the most comfortable way to get home. You will not be able to stay on higher levels when you get there through such negative emphasis.

No matter what high-minded rationalizations you comfort yourself with for coming back to earth, asceticism will keep bringing you back to the physical plane until you love enough to rise above it on a positive path. Indeed, it is love itself that *is* the positive path to space. There is no wisdom or holiness that is ever an excuse for the failure to love, in ourselves or others.

And in sexual relations, again, love overcomes the pendulum effect, the yin-yang of concepts, and at last we have a rational way to explain why love must be the first motive in sex. But love in this intention is much broader than romantic passion, and it must begin with loving yourself. If you love everything you feel and do, including your emotionally dry and empty moods, your pleasure will keep coming back. If you find sex unrewarding, it just means that in this lifetime or another you insisted too much on the other side of the balance. It is the action of contracting your awareness that makes any condition compulsory.

Also it is important not to judge others for their pleasures of the flesh. What you deny to others will be denied to you, for the plain reason that you are always legislating for yourself, all your words and actions define the world you want to live in. One of the necessary laws for our relations as equal beings is this: What you say, goes—but only for you

and those who agree with you. If you say a
man should not receive help undeservedly, it
may not affect his life much, but it will hold
for you: you will not get undeserved help. If
you say other people's sexual pleasures are
vulgar, it won't change their experiences, but
your pleasures will become vulgar. It is precisely your unlimited power to control your
experience that hangs you up. How much
compassion and forgiveness do you want for
yourself? Give it to others. Go to the extreme:
forgive all beings for their karmic debts to
you. Grant to others the freedom, the love,
the consciousness that you want for yourself.

Music shows us how to maintain pleasure
and ecstasy. Normally we tend to think of a
moment of euphoric realization as unbearable
and impossible to continue. It slips away and
then we pursue it again. It does so because we
are unwilling to let it go, we are unwilling to
conceive of being away from it. But if we take
the example of music, letting go of one note
to hear the next, then our pleasure can be
constant though the vibrations change.

If we "listen" to the world, and let it act
on us without either-or judgments and ideas,
then we can learn to comprehend each flash
of pleasure as a tone in the infinite harmony.
The orchestra of the world plays the familiar
melodies again and again, and the old folks
stand around and tap their feet while the
young ones dance.

CHAPTER FOUR

Lifesavers

Before going further, let's expand on some of
the basic attitudes salted away in what has
gone before. It is not my intention to have
anyone remember all the transistorized thinking in this book, but I highly recommend
memorizing the italic lines below. They are
simple enough to stay with you and will work
in any mental crisis. Keep them handy in your
mind.

One of my psychedelic excursions had
gotten off to a bad start, and I was sinking
into a really satanic bummer. As I looked
about me at people turning evil, shrunken,
colorless, old, and weird, I suddenly thought,
*"Well, what did you think it was that needed
to be loved?"* And just like that, the doors
opened and I was in paradise.

No resistance. This does not mean that you
must be physically passive or meekly put up
with bad vibrations or rip-offs. This means no
resistance in your mind. Be free in your head,
act out of love, and do what feels good. There
is no action that is always right or wrong: the
only true variable is the love with which you

act. As you open your awareness, life will improve of itself, you won't even have to try. It's a beautiful paradox: the more you open your consciousness, the fewer unpleasant events intrude themselves into your awareness.

Love as much as you can from wherever you are. This line is especially good to recall when you feel frightened, crazy, or have taken some bad dope. Write it on the wall of your room. You may not want to love what you feel or see, you may not be able to convince yourself that you could love it at all. But just decide to love it. Say out loud that you love it, even if you don't believe it. And say, "I love myself for hating this."

Love it the way it is. The way you see the world depends entirely on your own vibration level. When your vibration changes, the whole world will look different. It's like those days when everyone seems to be smiling at you because you feel happy. The way to raise your vibration level is to feel more love. Start by loving your negative feelings, your own boredom, dullness and despair. It's hard to believe, but changing the *content* of your mind does nothing to change your vibration level.

For the purpose of raising your awareness, it is useless to change your ideas, your faith, your behavior, your place of residence, or your companions.

It is not arbitrary nor an accident that you are where you are, so you might as well get your attitude straight before you make a change. Otherwise you might find yourself chasing all over creation looking for the right place, and not even the Sea of Infinite Bliss will feel right to you.

You take yourself with you wherever you go. As they say in Zen: If you can't find it where you're standing, where do you expect to wander in search of it? There is never anyplace in the universe to be except among your equals. The direction of change to seek is not in our four dimensions: it is getting deeper into what you are, where you are, like turning up the volume on the amplifier.

Love yourself. But isn't the definition of love being in the same space with *others?* Actually much of what we now think of as our selves— our bodies, our minds, our emotions—involves billions of other beings. Being the ego consciousness of a human body is a little like being Mayor of New York City. The ego is not the only awareness concerned with the survival or function of your body.

We are free, as individual, unique entities, to leave any group, such as the group that forms the body, but we will find other beings to harmonize with on any level we go to.

When you love your *self* you are in truth expanding in love into many other beings.

And the more loving you are, the more loving the beings within and around you. On all levels we are mutually dependent vibrations. Play a happy tune and happy dancers will join your trip.

In another sense, loving yourself is a willingness to be in the same space with your own creations. How contracted would you become if you try to withdraw from your own ideas?

Loving yourself is not a matter of building your ego. Egotism is proving you are worthwhile after you have sunk into hating yourself. Loving yourself will dissolve your ego: you will feel no need to prove you are superior.

CHAPTER FIVE
How we got here

We have a flood of ideas and names for many
different kinds of human behavior, but much
of what we do obeys certain common rules of
expansion and contraction. As I said, the rules
do not come from anywhere outside ourselves. If we conceive that we are equal beings,
then certain truths must follow about our
relationships with each other. We may call
these truths the source of fairness and justice,
but such names do not matter. It's just the
way it has to be if this universe of life is to
exist at all. It seems pointless to try to be convincing about this in words, compared to
what you will comprehend when you flash on
this divine order and justice for yourself when
you are meditating or high on psychedelics. I
can offer only limited speculation on how
these rules show up in our human experience.

The idea of equality has often been taken
to mean dropping to the lowest common
denominator, or settling for the characterless
common middle. Equality as I am suggesting
it is our coming together at the level of highest
awareness, pure space, without attachment or
resistance, with complete freedom of experi-

ence and consciousness, merging with others in whatever ecstasy or calm we choose. In all the vibration levels less than the highest, there are illusions of quantity and value, of greater and lesser love, intelligence, and powers. We appear to each other according to the vibrations we choose to emphasize, but we are equal in potential.

If that's true, how did we get so deep into mass that physical reality looks like the only reality? And that these comments on space sound like a peculiar and unverifiable fantasy? As concerns verification, I believe that the concept of equal entities can lead to a reintegration of currently available data in physics, and that we may then extrapolate from that information to describe the laws of our relations on a universal scale. Meanwhile I must indulge in some rough guesswork about how we got to the mass level in the first place.

We can start with a paradox at the highest level: expanded beings, completely unresisting, are also completely irresistible. Space beings are entirely permissive to other beings, but when one of us contracts, he becomes dense to the extent of his contraction, and is then in appearance *propelled* by the space beings. The experience of being propelled and later compelled is due entirely to the density of the contracted beings. Space beings have no intention to propel or compel anyone to do anything.

All conceivable universes in all conceivable dimensions exist in the One Mind as pure idea or archetype. When any of us withdraws from a *willingness* to create any aspect of that, we drop to a lower vibration level. For this illustration, imagine we are a great number of energy beings who are indifferent to the idea of Pluto the Dog. Since we are denser than space beings, they would propel us, and we would appear in space as a flowing, flashing image of Pluto the Dog, looking like a fireworks display, perhaps.

Imagine, then, some of us, more than indifferent, who *deny* the concept of Pluto the Dog, withdrawing to the mass level. Our mass, being even denser than the energy, is compelled to take the form denied, and behold the physical manifestation of Pluto the Dog. In this manner, what is denied on the conceptual level, the space level, becomes manifest on the physical plane.

Of course, the truth is not quite that cut-and-dried, but it will give you the idea. Space appears to propel energy, and energy appears to compel matter. But these reactions cannot occur without the density of the more withdrawn beings. By denying your capacity to create a concept, or by denying someone else's freedom to do so, you drop to a vibration where not only Pluto the Dog is evident, but a lot of other material forms also. Denying the truth is what opens Pandora's box.

You don't have to assume that you personally denied every miserable thing that happens on earth: when you deny coffee you also become compulsively involved with the reality of tea and cocoa. There was *something* that freaked you, or more likely a whole series of ideas that you were unwilling to conceive of or love, so that gradually your vibrations dropped to a mass level, and you found yourself being a body. But there's nothing holding you down to a mass level, regardless of all your experiences of being pushed and pulled by other masses, by energy, and by space. It's your own ignorance, your density, that makes it possible for you to be pushed. You can't feel pain until you're stupid. Pain is the experience of not being able to get into the same space with others.

But all you need do to get free of pain, to get un-stupid, is to be *willing* to be aware of anything that enters your consciousness.

There are many events closer to earth in which we can see the compulsion-by-denial process working. Of all the paradoxes with which we struggle on the material level, the failure of good intentions is perhaps one of the most baffling. Good people try to do good things and get bad results. Peaceful youths are jailed, spiritual communes are attacked, and flower children become bombers. Often in history spiritual revivals have been followed by bloodshed and persecution. Perhaps we can now understand why these things happen.

What you cannot think about, you cannot control. What you cannot conceive of in your awareness, you will stumble over in your path. Violent human beings are precisely those who refuse at some time to conceive that they could be violent. It also happens that if you are unwilling to conceive of people being the victims of violence, you may become a victim yourself, for you will not be sufficiently aware of how it happens to avoid it. Everything that is manifest begins in the spirit: every evil that is manifest to us is there because we refused to conceive of causing it, or denied someone else the freedom to conceive of it. The way out, as hard as it may be to believe, is not by resisting further, by moving the furniture around, but by being willing to conceive of it—by loving it, in short. As we should have done in the first place.

Unfortunately, most people with good intentions are trying to deny or eliminate what is already manifest. And many spiritual revivals are a deeper denial of the facts of our vibration level.

What can we do about evil? A great deal, if our heads are clear. My catch-all phrase is: "I wouldn't deny *that* experience to the One Mind."

Once you have cleared your head on the matter, then do whatever feels right to you.

Evil occurs as a secondary reality, after you have withdrawn to a low vibration level. The seduction of evil is precisely in that it involves us in trying to eliminate it.

When your consciousness is open, any action you take in reference to evil has no more significance than digging a ditch to channel floodwaters away from a house. By all means, go to the doctor when you are sick; disable someone trying to hurt you; ask unpleasant people to leave your house; start a revolution: just keep your awareness open all the while, and know that your evil has manifested itself in your life because of your lack of love. The true enemy, if there is one, is in yourself, in your failure to love enough. But there is no moral judgment in our involvement with evil. If you refuse to admit that automobiles exist, you're going to get hit by cars, not because you are sinful or neurotic, but just because you are not looking at automobiles. You won't see them coming.

Some people think that "thoughts are things" and that you must avoid negative thoughts or they will happen. As we have seen earlier, thoughts are certainly powerful when conceived by expanded beings. But trying to withdraw from thoughts is what got us incarnated on a mass level in the first place. If you avoid negative thoughts, they will sooner or later manifest themselves physically. It is your resistance to the negative thought, whether you bring it to consciousness or not, that makes it manifest in your life.

What am I doing on a level of conscious-ness where this is real? That is the first ques-tion to ask yourself when you become aware of something ugly or evil or stupid. We are always in a context of our equals, and the justice of love is always perfect. The universe is an infinite tapestry of perfectly ordered love relationships, and when you are loving enough, you rise. It's not even a matter of waiting until your lifetime is over. Your movement as a being is not horizontal through time, so to speak. All states of consciousness are available right now. Every possibility in the past and future exists timelessly, it's always there, and you activate your level of reality by your own vibrations.

There is a jewel of perfect ecstasy of being who you are. You are at the level of consciousness that has the greatest pleasure and ecstasy you are capable of accepting. Regardless of what I tell myself, or what I have at times experienced, my greatest plea-sure right now is to be penniless in a room in San Francisco writing this book.

Try these sayings during meditation: *I surrender to this reality. I have no resistance to this reality. I am one with this reality. I surrender to the justice of our equality. I have no resistance to the justice of our equality. I am one with the justice of our equality.*

CHAPTER SIX

Self-improvement

I hope you will find it encouraging to learn
how these general ideas apply to eliminating
evils in yourself, to spiritual self-improvement.
The more bad thoughts and feelings you try
to weed out of yourself, the more there will be.

Since I myself have certain preferences
for what I want to do, I must be wary of
passing these on as having the dignity of law.
Therefore I must necessarily become even
more personal in this chapter, and make my
bias clear. I *am* lazy, and it bothers me to see
people strenuously pursuing self-improvement
goals by methods that will not work, and
urging me to do the same. They are often the
loveliest of people, and I would love to join
them if I thought they would succeed. On the
other hand, perhaps they *know* the goal will
never be reached by their means, and I am the
fool for exposing what everyone secretly
knows. If we didn't have these games, that
would leave a Void, wouldn't it? I am playing
the game of refusing pointless games, which
may be the most pointless of all.

Obviously there is a danger here of wan-
dering in circles, but if someone else knew

what was in this chapter, I would want him to tell me, so I must take a small risk.

A structure is any relation between entities that avoids dissolving. The self that you know as a human being is a structure, an organization of billions of entities.

An odd thing about structures is that they will dissolve both from success and failure, so the problem, if you want a structure, is to maintain a tension somewhere between the two.

The idea that structures will disintegrate when completely successful struck me as peculiar, and I made a list of hasty examples: a victorious empire inevitably breaks up into parts or collapses when it reaches its peak and is unopposed. A man inherits wealth and "ruins" himself with dissipation. The genius goes insane. "Power corrupts." "The good die young." Religions break into schisms and heresies. A dominant species mysteriously becomes extinct. A cell divides in two. The magician goes mad.

Hence people are cautious about success or power too easily gained. On some level, the structure invokes a self-imposed limit on success, including success in pursuing spiritual awareness. Spiritual leaders keep telling us the ego must die to be reborn, but we hold back. The structure preserves itself.

The ego, the mental structure, "feels better" when it has to contend with the tension of threats to itself. We feel "high" and energetic when tested by negative possibilities: hard work, discipline, sky-diving, racing, wars (until Vietnam—the North Vietnamese got high off that one—the U.S. didn't because it wasn't threatened), illness, fasting, asceticism, gambling, drugs, careless driving, arguing, paranoia (invented threats), contending with the devil and black magic, and so on.

Of course, if the negative definition goes too far, the structure will collapse, but somehow that doesn't bother us. We love to worry about dangers to human survival. (Unless it is a real one, like the atomic bomb or germ warfare. Then the risk is "unreal," we are reluctant to think about it.)

As a normal process, we define ourselves, we find out who we are, by what we disagree with. And we identify others by what is wrong with them: we keep looking until we find some difference between "us" and "them." Virtues in others are invisible, not really interesting.

We human beings, almost alone among species, have solved the problem of maintaining negative tension by being our own worst enemies. We can never completely overcome "human nature" in ourselves or others, so the game goes on. It is plain that we are getting a reward from all the ghastly facts of life we complain of: that's what sells newspapers.

Negative emphasis results in an intensified structure and a stronger ego. Even though some of these activities, like self-denial, are carried on under the banner of spiritual search, the result is the same. On a subtle level we know that most spiritual endeavors will not succeed, but we go on maintaining the fantasy that they are admirable. Many of us have no intention of *really* succeeding in dissolving our attachment to structure and going to another plane of existence.

But what of those, wise and serious, who zealously pursue enlightenment by traditional methods? Since we know that negative methods of getting high will not lead to a stable experience of space, what is it that makes yoga rewarding?

The reason yoga works when it does is in the love expressed between teacher and student, and in the student's willing placement of attention. If you limit your experience to phenomena you are completely willing to conceive of, such as the contents of a cave in Tibet, you will certainly get high sooner or later.

But as soon as you walk out of the cave, you will find people behaving just as they did before. And if you are not willing to be the cause of their behavior, and love them as they are, your vibration level will drop. And then you may preach about how evil the world is, how corrupt cities are, how sinful people are.

Insofar as we are seriously concerned

about evil, not just as a negative-tension game, we should see that we need not be concerned with evil as a *physical* manifestation: it is that such manifestations have their source in space-level concepts that exist in timeless possibility. It is as a *concept* that evil is real and is always within us. If we cannot learn how to deal with it on earth, we will be plagued with it even in heaven.

Even if you are not just testing your structure, the *motive* for purifying yourself —that you feel spiritually impure—will prevent any genuine gain until you learn to love the impurity you started with. Can any being seriously think that he is going to pass through the infinity of time without ever making another mistake?

Quite often a flash of enlightenment will give you this message: Go back to where you started and learn to love it more.

There is another handicap to conventional methods of self-elevation: If you identify with a status system of spiritual values, it can produce unloving snobbery towards your brothers. The justice of our relations is exact, and if you are unloving the results will manifest explicitly. You may then complain, "If I'm working so hard to be pure, why do these things happen, why do people hate me?" But there is no purity greater than love, even when it is corrupt and unwashed.

The positive way to define your ego is to

be one with the cause of it: love it the way it is, then freely choose whatever behavior feels good to you. You won't blow away; you can experience your present structure as a space-level interaction, and then go higher only if you want to.

Changing your vibration level, raising your love level, is the only action that results in a real change for the better. Group encounters, sexual freedom, revolution, yoga, diets, asceticism, rock music, dope, all means are dependent on your interest and creative power to be effective. These are all good games, but don't try to force yourself past the time when you are really interested. They work only while your attention to them is aroused. And when they work too well, too successfully, you are likely to "lose interest." When you feel your structure turning into energy and then space, you are likely to pull back, unless you accept what is happening and stabilize at a new level.

There really are more loving games than improving yourself or reforming other people, or otherwise using negative tension to harden your structure.

Keep in mind that your survival does not depend on any structure. You are a unity, an entity just like all the others in the universe. When you ain't got nothin', you got nothin' to lose.

There isn't anything "wrong" with using

negative events to define your ego, as long as you do it consciously, because you want to. The only wrongness in any activity is being withdrawn from awareness of what you are doing. We can play these same silly games with a lot more pleasure when we are aware of what we are really doing.

When you offer people spiritual solutions —or solutions of any kind for anything, for that matter—you are asking them to give up what makes them feel active, alive, defined— their ego structure. Be careful—*it's dangerous!*

Well, just for starters, take it that every human being is a perfect whatever-it-is right now. Every state of consciousness is perfect and complete, and does not need to be changed. And every change of consciousness is perfect and complete, and does not need to be static.

I have tried to cover all the possibilities at once with a couple of maxims:

Whether I am conscious of it or not, I am one with the cause of all that exists.

Whether I feel it or not, I am one with all the love in the universe.

CHAPTER SEVEN

Time and vibrations

We can vary our experience of time by changing our vibrations, just as we alter our perception of the rest of the physical universe. Our concepts, feelings, and limited relations have beginnings and endings in time, but we do not. On the space level, when we are completely expanded, the time is always now.

When you look at a lake, there is no water in your mind. Put another way, the awareness of a hard object has no hardness in it. The awareness of confusion is not confused. The awareness of insanity is not insane. The awareness of the passage of time takes no time, there is no time in it.

We "measure" time by the compulsive repetition of interactions on the mass level. And the more expanded our consciousness, the less compulsion we are involved in. Our subjective awareness of time is often at variance with the clock.

Many of us by now are familiar with distortions of time when high on marijuana, and of course the stronger psychedelics go to greater extremes. How does this happen? A brief guess at the sources of the time experience is highly worth while, because it suggests how practical it is to look to your own vibration level before reacting to what you think is an external reality.

Think of perception as a kind of radar: your wave goes out and bounces back from an object. Needless to say, the facts are more complex than this illustration, but it's close enough to serve.

Let's say someone is shaking a table and a cup is starting to slide off. If your perceptual vibrations are very slow, your waves will give you one message about where the cup is when it starts falling, another flash when it is halfway to the floor, and another when it hits. But if you are vibrating quickly, you will get many messages as the cup starts to fall, telling you the direction it is going, and you will feel as though you have plenty of time to reach over and catch it if you want to.

Note carefully that when your vibrations are slow, events seem to happen fast, and you will feel that events are happening too fast for you to control them. And you may therefore feel impelled to try that much harder to exercise control. You may try to establish habits of orderly behavior, and you may resent disorderly people. This is one origin of the power trip. You may try to get away from disturbing events by moving to the country, or turn off your consciousness with hard drugs or liquor.

But the faster you are vibrating and the more messages you get back from your environment, the slower events will appear to be happening, and the more you will feel you are in control. The more you love, the faster you vibrate, then the less need you feel to control anything, and you are not fearful of change and variety. You experience everything deeper and slower and more lovingly.

The higher the ratio of expansion to contraction in yourself, the more expanded and loving you are, the faster you vibrate.

The secondary reality is useful in the sense that it will always give you a clear picture of your vibration level. If the world looks beautiful and safe, you are vibrating fast; if it looks gloomy, dull, or frightening, then you are vibrating slow, and you need to love yourself for vibrating too slow.

Inside yourself or outside, you never have to change what you see, only the way you see it. It is useless to try to escape any difficulty by contracting your consciousness. You will have to climb back up any hill you roll down, you will have to do it sooner or later, in this lifetime or another, because our true nature is beyond time.

Never pull your attention away from a scene impulsively because it looks ugly, unpleasant, or painful.

Make a conscious decision, the words are enough, to love yourself for seeing it as revolting. If possible, keep your attention on it until it turns beautiful, or at least until you are indifferent to it.

You don't have to go looking for bad scenes to test yourself, or remind yourself of all that is wrong in the world, but once a scene manifests itself in your presence, become as fully aware of it as you can.

Staying with it is important. You may hide in your room or leave the city, but *you* as an entity will still be stuck on a low vibration level of denial if you pull away suddenly. It will seem like the strangest of coincidences when, having withdrawn your attention sharply from one unpleasant scene, you keep running into others like it. That will baffle you, and keep happening until you come to an unpleasantness you can tolerate or love, and your vibrations go up.

Look at it, love it, and *then* get away! It's all right to channel your attention to what is pleasant for you. What else is freedom for? And as long as there is free will, there are always going to be some beings creating vibrations you do not like, no matter what level you are on. The point is to take your leave in a way that doesn't hang you up.

After a few experiences with loving weird events, you will be tuned in enough to get early warning when someone is likely to rip you off or otherwise stir up bad vibrations, (when the cup is starting to fall, so to speak,) and you will be able to make the right moves before it gets too involved.

Don't feel that it is "unspiritual" to perceive unwholesome possibilities in other people: it isn't paranoia if the object of your fear is real.

It's just carelessness karma if you ignore early warnings. Keep your mind open and unresisting to any possibility: that's what gives you the information to keep evil from manifesting in your life. Pay attention, here and now. It's all right to say No.

No matter what others are doing, you are the only one who is responsible for what happens to you. There is nothing in the external event that in the least way determines your feelings and experiences: your life is entirely governed by your vibrations, what they tell you and how you respond.

The slower your vibrations, the more unpleasant your life: you will contend with more conflict, mass, and pain. Events will happen too fast for control, yet time will seem interminable because you can see no way out.

But when you raise your vibration level, you can neatly sidestep collisions, both psychic and physical, and quite literally change the world for the better. Love is the strongest magic of all.

When you learn to love hell, you will be in heaven.

CHAPTER EIGHT

Going through changes

If nothing is holding us down to the physical
plane, then what's holding us? Why are we
attached to structures? Why do we stick to
our vibration level? Why do we fear change?

To answer these questions, let's start at
the top once again. There are a lot of words
for how it feels to be completely expanded:
total awareness, completeness, freedom, love,
ecstasy, certainty, stability, supreme intelligence, compassion. I think it will be least
vague in this instance to discuss our interactions in terms of stability.

Absolute stability exists naturally at the
space level, because *all relationships are persistent to the degree that the beings involved
have the same expansion.*

But on the more contracted levels, where
there is by definition some withdrawal of
awareness, we accordingly have less control
over how long the stable condition lasts. And
when we are relating to beings whose vibrations are higher or lower than ours, we feel
unstable and uncertain.

In an unstable relationship, we have
basically two ways to go, regardless of the

subtleties of the changes: one way is towards stability, reaching a common level of vibration; the other way is towards disintegration, getting so far apart in vibrations that we are no longer aware of each other at all. Since we are uncomfortable in the presence of vibrations higher or lower than our own, we tend to make certain "natural" responses. If the other person is lower, we will generally try to get him up to our level, to help him and cheer him up. But if the other person is higher, we will often, at first, try to bring him down and get him to lower his vibrations. Note that when you try to help someone you are working against his natural, perhaps unconscious effort to bring you down. The lower vibrating person (and this could be any of us depending on the circumstance) will appear to be draining the energy of the higher person, often with the best moral and social motives. This effort can take the form of exaggerated praise, sly pokes disguised in polite words, pleading for help with problems, showing fear and depression, freaking out, starting an argument, quoting better authorities, and a thousand other forms, all the way down to putting the higher person in prison or killing him.

On the other end, if you are faced with such behavior, the remedy is to keep on outflowing love, to have no resistance in your mind. The lower vibrating person may reach farther and farther to bring you down, but when he finds you will not come down, when he senses that you have no internal resistance to him, he will have to rise to your vibration level to feel stable and comfortable, it is too painful to stay where he is. And he *will* rise, unless of course he goes the other way, and disintegrates from the relationship. You are not, however, obliged to wait him out: if you sense that he is not going to do anything but try to bring you down, you are free to effect the disintegration when you choose. In current language, just split. Don't dwell on it, and don't feel guilty about it. It's in the natural order of things.

If you are going to take psychedelics or meditate and open yourself to communication with beings on higher levels, you should be aware of the implications of these automatic interactions between vibration levels. You are likely to feel overwhelmed, driven, compelled, degraded, full of psychic terror (the bummer) until you drop your resistance, expand in love, and move up to the vibration of the higher beings. They have no intention to scare you or test you, it's your own density that is making you have those feelings.

Anything that really frightens you may contain a clue to enlightenment. It may indicate to you how deeply you are attached to structure, whether mental, physical, or social. Attachment and resistance are appearances with the same root: when you resist by pulling away your awareness, the emotion is one of fear, and the contraction is experienced as a pull like magnetism or gravity; that is, attachment.

That is why we often fear to open our minds to more exalted spiritual beings. We think fear is a signal to withdraw, when in fact it is a sign we are already withdrawing too much.

Here are some lines that have made me feel good, both in times of emotional turmoil and in meditation:

I am nothing, I am empty, I am silent.

I have no resistance to the vibrations of other beings.

I have no resistance to the expansions and contractions of other beings.

When we are afraid to see what is higher, we may then try to buy a feeling of safety or power by keeping our attention on what is lower. This process takes many forms in human life.

Charity conceived as an impulse towards those lower than ourselves often has unhappy results. Many of our impulsive feelings have their source in erroneous assumptions about the status of other people. There is nothing wrong with feelings—the feelings on the space level are incredibly rich. But it is wise to pay attention to where our feelings are coming from, and where they are leading us. We may be seduced by a feeling of freedom, power, or amusement by relating to those we think are weaker; or we may recoil from the fear and depression we feel in the presence of those we consider stronger.

The principle of equality is a safe guide, both in saving us from foolish condescension to disturbed people, and from self-limiting awe towards superior people.

The solution to all our push-pull tensions is to treat everyone, every being you recognize to be alive, as equal to yourself. Always look deeper than any evidence that you are unequal. If another person displays great wisdom or genius, produces great paintings, or even inflates himself to writing books of advice like this one, just DON'T BELIEVE it is any evidence that his potential is higher than yours. Know that anything he has done, you can do—not in the sense of debasing him but of elevating yourself. Don't "admire" him excessively—that separates you. Let him be what he is, love him as your brother, enjoy what he produces, treat him as an equal. And whatever you see on a psychedelic trip, just say, *"I'm equal to that; we are all equal to that."*

On the other side, if a person displays sickness and insanity, degradation and emotional distress, helplessness and despair, just don't believe it is any evidence that his potential is lower than yours. Know that anything you are doing, he can do. Don't blindly agree with his game; don't react as though what he is doing is real. Let him be what he is, love him as your brother, have compassion for him, treat him as your equal. Begin with the knowledge that he can bring himself out of it. Don't ignore him necessarily, unless you know that he has been running the same movie over and over and are bored with it. Your attention is always life-giving; it will make him feel stable and loved, and he can go up from there *if* he wants to. You can even tell him in words that you don't believe his game: do it while you are bandaging his wounds or feeding him or giving him money. Don't act superior to him: you aren't, you're his equal. Ignore the sin and love the sinner.

It is not a personal affront to you when someone is being discordant, it is a measure of his pain. He's showing you how much he hurts, and how much compassion he needs. But keep in mind, too, that not all victims are innocent. In a certain karmic sense, no victims are innocent, but that doesn't mean we shouldn't help them, for it is our fate to exist in a relation to them, and how we behave determines our own karma. But we should give help in a way that does not extend our attachment to low vibrations. That means we should give what we would expect to get, good or bad, in the same circumstance, and begin with the knowledge that all beings are equals.

While we still believe there are people greater or lesser than ourselves, we will tend to hang on all the more tightly to our current vibration level, we will be fastened to the people who make us feel at home. We will be stuck with our ideas, our emotional habits, our jobs, our bodies. We will be afraid to change because we will fear the unstable experiences we have when we try to reach a "higher" level. We will be afraid of falling to a "lower" level if we let go of our current stability.

Once you begin to behave in the knowledge that no being is greater or lesser than you, then you are free to change, because you will feel stable no matter what level you are on. You will feel calm and sure of yourself with or without a body, with or without a job, a brain, a book to read, or a book to write.

Withdrawing awareness from the expansions of others, and keeping attention on the contractions of others, fastens us to the world of matter. It is reassuring to know that this process, which got us incarnated in bodies in the first place, is also happening in our daily lives, and can be reversed very easily, starting now.

It is a nice truth that the way that will relieve your woes on the physical plane will also take you to the highest spiritual realizations. And the way is simple: *No resistance.*

CHAPTER NINE

What is real?

The concept that we live in a universe of
equal beings can make sense of all religions,
and can contain all metaphysical attitudes. It
is the easiest raft to discard when we reach
the other shore that is no shore. It can tell us
how to live on this plane, it can integrate our
scientific knowledge, it can show how our
physical existence is the expression of spiritual
laws. It gives us an absolutely confident understanding of what is true and what is real.

Equal and unique live beings are all that
is fully true and real in the universe. We *are*
the universe.

We experience the deepest sense of
reality only at the highest expansion in perfect
love. On lower vibration levels, we see other
beings relating to each other in a way that is
not entirely true or real.

For a down-to-earth example, let us consider that the people in an audience are real,
but "audience" is a name for something that
will disappear when the people go home. In
this sense, the audience is an illusion: a temporary, partial and limited reality—it has no
independent, causative existence.

We can construct a statistical probability about how the audience will behave, but each member is free to come and go at will, just as the atoms forming our bodies come and go. It is in this meaning that we can say that the physical universe, including our bodies, is an illusion.

We are real: the beings participating in the universe—us, the particles in the atoms, the energy and space beings, all are real, all are equal, all are of one kind.

But the relationships, groupings and massings are illusory as we see them from any given vibration level. Thus, as the audience is formed of people, illusions are formed out of real beings. Indeed, there is no other way to form an illusion except by using what is real, there is no other material around.

However, rather than speak of the world as illusory, which can be interpreted as a license to steal and be otherwise unloving, and can only be annoying when you feel stuck where you are, it is better to call it a secondary reality. The world is real enough when we are vibrating within a particular range, but *only* while we are doing so.

Facts are limited truths: the way relationships between others look to us when we have limited our own awareness and love, or when they have limited theirs. But facts have roots in the truth: we may have only a limited view of the beings involved in what we see as matter, but those beings are real, they are self-determined and are acting in harmony.

However, we don't need facts to be wise and loving. Different sets of facts are real at different vibration levels. The truth is the same for everyone, the facts are always a little different for everyone.

Facts are certainly fascinating, like gossip: who's doing what to whom, what's doing what to what. Of the gathering of facts there is no end. Sometimes we feel that if we had enough of them, we could get at the truth. Sometimes we madly try to deny them even though we are attached to a vibration level from which they will not disappear.

Illusions, facts, are reliable to the extent that they have truth in them, but they are also somewhat delusory.

Delusions are denials of the truth. If we use the physical plane to deny higher reality, we are deluded. But if we deny the reality that is in the material world, we are deluded also. We cannot rise above the physical plane by denying its reality: we must love it and affirm the reality of the live beings who form it.

Some of us grow discouraged with spiritual efforts because enlightening experiences don't always help us handle the facts of physical existence any better. We may even mess up more: an LSD trip may show us how vaporous the world is, and then we get annoyed because hard, mass-level reality is still there when we come down.

Enlightening experiences can help in dealing with facts by showing you that you are a completely flexible whatever-it-is, capable of existing on many different vibration levels, both within and above the physical plane.

Once you know that the facts will be different on every level, you are less likely to fight the facts of any particular plane. As your awareness opens up, you will be able to choose the level you want, and you will have more enjoyable facts to deal with.

There is no being in the universe more powerful than you, but there are also none less powerful than you. This should be the starting point of all your behavior towards other people. I often say to myself: *Let my intentions not attempt to contradict the necessary laws of our relations as equal beings.* (A long sentence, but I do say it.)

Since every being is self-determined, you cannot change anyone else's vibration level against his will, nor are you obliged to. You cannot in reality hurt or help others without their agreement to play the game, nor can anyone hurt or help you without your agreement.

Indeed, your perception of others is colored by your own limited vibrations until you reach the higher levels, so you have no way of knowing exactly what it is you are trying to change. On the other hand, you do control your own vibration level absolutely, and that's all the freedom you need to govern your own relationships and experiences.

You are free to be anywhere you want to be in the world that is real to you now. And beyond that, you are capable of being in any time, on any vibration level, in any system, with whomever you like.

Regardless of how trapped you feel, how weighed down by one day after another, your fundamental freedom is not affected.

If you look at your environment now, you may see a great deal of "reality" that makes you feel secure even when it hurts or tires you out. It's all right to hold onto that while you think this over. Nothing is going to happen unexpectedly just as a result of reading about how free you are.

In any case, you're never alone—there are many beings aware of you at all times, loving you, ready to make you feel it whenever you are ready to open up to it, taking care to see that you don't get in too deep, encouraging you to love yourself.

The world you see is in truth a reality of convenience—in a sense, the universe will compassionately arrange itself into anything you need it to be to work out your preferences. You have an infinite choice of worlds to live in.

You are also free to live according to many different cosmic plans. The fact that you can choose doesn't make any one of them less valid. You may live in a universe in which there is a God at the top, with a hierarchy down to souls in outer darkness. Or a materialistic world in which you experience no life after death, just a complete wipe-out of the past. You may have a heaven and hell.

Whatever your choice, whatever vibrations feel right to you, you will tune in and stabilize with others believing the same thing. On the space level, like usually attracts like.

You can tune your vibrations to Christ consciousness or Buddha consciousness and experience supernal compassion. You can tune yourself to black magic and live in a world of weird shapes and violent forces. You can tune in on Mickey Mouse or Mr. Natural in the cosmic comic book. You can become one with the Divine Mother and dwell in incredible sensuous luxury.

You may have all these experiences and more when you meditate or take psychedelics. You may not remember this book then, but you will be able to remember two words: *No resistance*. These two words apply even more importantly on those levels than on this one, if anything. Remember them especially when you are dying.

Since we aren't going anywhere, with stability, any faster than our love will take us,

and we have to love it where we are first,
there is something to be said for not getting
too ambitious about the infinite possibilities.

But it's nice to know that there is more
to it than what you see in front of you now,
and that you can experience your present
reality on much deeper levels of pleasure and
ease.

CHAPTER TEN

How you get there

There are many paths to enlightenment. Some of us who have expanded to a degree of illumination have thereafter preached the dogmatic certainty of one particular path.

But enlightenment doesn't care how you get there. And if you aren't going to be thinking about it in paradise, then don't worry about it now.

My suggestions intend only to show why you must actually do it yourself. Act from what you know to be true. My own attitude, arrived at with an excess of labor and doubt, is that I will not settle for any path that makes it difficult for most people as I know them to be, or perhaps excludes them entirely for lifetimes to come.

For myself, I must take the path that is available to everyone. When I get there by LSD or other paths, I find myself coming back to help those who are not spiritual athletes. By taking the path open to all, I will know that those who have stayed behind are doing so of their own free will, and I won't have to come back again.

As there is perfect enlightenment, so

there is a perfect means to enlightenment: a simple path that is available to every being in the universe *all the time.* Love is the perfect means to enlightenment. It is available at all times to every being: nothing, no one has the power to stand in the way.

And as soon as you choose to take the path that is available to everyone, that's it: you are *on* the path that is available to everyone.

This book revolves around the hypothesis in the first paragraph of Chapter One, but let it be clear that I have many times actually been in all the states of consciousness discussed, as have many other human beings. I'm not just guessing. These states are no farther from us than a breath of air. And often I have had to let go of this concept itself, and can therefore say with confidence: Go beyond reason to love—it is safe. It is the only safety. Love all you can, and when you are ready all will be shown to you.

The state of mind that most needs enlightenment is the one that sees human beings as *needing* to be guided or enlightened.

The sin that most needs to be loved and forgiven is the state of mind that sees human beings as sinners.

Those of us who arrive at a flash of space through a negative emphasis may try to comfort ourselves that we are on a Bodhisattva trip, coming down to help others. But we should be then even more discriminating of our motives.

Every person who allows others to treat him as a spiritual leader has the responsibility to ask himself: Out of all the perceptions available to me in the universe, why am I emphasizing the ignorance of my brothers? What am I doing in a role where this is real? What kind of standards am I conceiving, in which so many people are seen to be in suffering, while I am the enlightened one?

These questions came to me with a great shock, and this is one way I might answer for myself: Everything that is happening in your body is happening on an infinite range of vibration levels. If you love your lack of information better than I love this knowledge, then you are on a higher level than I. There is absolutely no external evidence that will tell me how much you love yourself, because I am seeing you with the limited vision of my own vibrations. In that sense, what I see is myself.

No matter how confused or stupid or unloving other persons may appear to us, we have no right ever to assume that their consciousness is on a lower level than ours. They may be realizing far deeper dimensions of love. The way we see them is an explicit measure of our own vibration level.

The very people we now see as vulgar, unenlightened, stupid, rip-offs, insane—these people, when we learn to love them *and all our feelings about them*, are our tickets to paradise. And that is all we need to do—love them. We may express that love or not as we wish, in any way we wish. It doesn't even matter how we treat them. But we must see them and love them as they are now, for we cannot deny them the freedom to be what they are, just as we must love ourselves as we are now.

Let us remember that each person is some kind of opposite of what he insisted on in the past or could be in the future. As long as we conceive of ourselves as limited beings, we are all the same distance from the center, whether we are good or bad, sane or mad.

If a man has some awareness of higher levels and knows that he is free to be any- where in the universe, he may then seek to justify taking part in a physical game. The most self-flattering way to disguise his appe- tite is to see himself as a bringer of enlighten- ment, of purity, of virtue. No one, not even he, will question his motives and results: isn't he doing what he says he is doing? If others fail to reach his height, it's not his fault—and thus he keeps the game going forever. It's self-renewing as long as he is unwilling to see that his own vibrations emphasize the evil and ignorance he sees. The more he hates evil, the more evil there is to hate. The more he advises people to resist the material world the more he binds them to it.

And even these comments are the consequence of my own resistance to the "error" of resisting evil. This is a perfect example of how we are always guilty of what we condemn in others. What we see is always ourselves. It is useless to correct anyone's behavior. If he knew what he was doing, he wouldn't be doing it, true enough, but he is just as capable of knowing it as we are. If he doesn't see it of his own free will, is he any more likely to do so when we tell him? By denying him his freedom to be wrong, we are equally wrong. Giving others the freedom to be stupid is one of the most important and hardest steps to take in spiritual progress. Conveniently the opportunity to take that step is all around us every day.

Those of us who pretend to greater knowledge than our brothers, who report more enlightened experiences, have more to explain precisely because we know more.

This book is the description and education of my own ignorance. And beyond the information herein, I am trying to show how a human being can handle the kind of experiences I have had without laying strange trips on his brothers and sisters. Whenever we hand on what we are shown, we must do so with the same divine love with which it was shown to us. We are but channels of spiritual joy, and to continue to have it we need only be open channels.

If we always stand facing the higher light, like looking into the sun, our vision of the people around us will be distorted. But if we have the light coming over our shoulders, shining through us, we will see the beauty of others, we will be open to the light coming through all forms, and know the glory of the creation.

And I say it often: *Thank you, brothers and sisters, for letting my consciousness be in this place.*

While we have humility and pride enough to act on the knowledge that we exist in an infinite harmony, that we are neither greater nor lesser than any others, we can enjoy exquisite spiritual wealth and pleasures.

Let every jewel remind you of the diamond light of love. Know that the smallest kindness is a facet in the infinite jewel of enlightenment.

A Fable

Once upon a time there dwelt an old King in a palace. In the center of a golden table in the main hall, there shone a large and magnificent jewel. Each day of the King's life, the stone sparkled more resplendently.

One day a thief stole the jewel and ran from the palace, hiding in a forest. As he stared with deep joy at the stone, to his amazement the image of the King appeared in it.

"I have come to thank you," said the King. "You have released me from my attachment to Earth. I thought I was freed when I acquired the jewel, but then I learned that I would be released only when I passed it on, with a pure heart, to another.

"Each day of my life I polished that stone, until finally this day arrived, when the jewel became so beautiful that you stole it, and I have passed it on, and am released.

"The jewel you hold is Understanding. You cannot add to its beauty by hiding it and hinting that you have it, nor yet by wearing it with vanity. Its beauty comes of the consciousness that others have of it. Honor that which gives it beauty."

Even Lazier

A selection of reminders from the text:

We are equal beings and the universe
is our relations with each other.

What am I doing on a level of consciousness
where this is real?

No resistance.

Love it the way it is.

Love as much as you can from
wherever you are.

Whether I am conscious of it or not, I am
one with the cause of all that exists.

Whether I feel it or not, I am one with
all the love in the   universe.

Love is the only dimension that needs
to be changed.

Go beyond reason to love: it is safe.
It is the only safety.

All states of consciousness are
available right now.

It's always within us to relate this way.

Enlightenment doesn't care how
you get there.

Whatever you are doing, love yourself
for doing it.

There is nothing you need to do first
in order to be enlightened.

This, too, can be experienced with
a completely expanded awareness.

I wouldn't deny this experience to
the One Mind.

What did you think it *was* that needed
to be loved?

When you learn to love hell, you will
be in heaven.

Thank you, brothers and sisters, for
letting my consciousness be in this place.